"This book presents basic truths for re-establishing a woman's worth. It is astounding that something so basic has been attacked so strategically by the enemy with the aid of warped societal inferences. I believe when we allow a person to determine our value we have already shortchanged ourselves, therefore nullifying our ability to fully pay the bill of our destiny. Dejah Fields' transparency allows for readers to see themselves through her experience with a hope that inspires change. I encourage you to read this book to determine that you cancel rejection, low self-esteem, and abandonment, and through forgiveness demand the freedom of the Lord."
—*Riva Tims, Senior Pastor Majestic Life Church, Orlando FL*

"I felt like Dejah was in my living room, speaking to me from her heart. She has a strong gift of encouragement, mixed with a heavy dose of reality as well as a healthy trust in God and His promises. It's a shame that many women will relate to this book and its pain; it's a blessing that they will receive encouragement and direction from it."
—*Mike Stangel, Senior Pastor, North Shore Christian Fellowship, Haleiwa, Hawaii*

"This book takes a candid and intimate look at the underlying and negative emotions that plague and limit women from being all what God has created them to be! With such personal stories and insight, it is apparent that Dejah has gone through and experienced the joy and power of understanding her journey! She takes you on a journey that will relate, connect, and provide you understanding as to why many women voluntarily lose their identity in life. When you read this book, it will awaken you to understand the deceptions while leading you to truth, peace, and freedom of knowing who you are!"
—*Michele DeCaul, Life Strategist—EMERGE! Life Coaching*

"I believe this book will inspire woman not only to find their true identity but also their healing in the Word of God. It offers men an insight into what their daughters and wives feel and experience, and reminds them of their divine purpose, as fathers and husbands, to treat women honorably."
—*Leonard D. Daniels, Minister/national recording artist*
JUSTUS Records

"One thing you will find when reading this book is that it's a book that will push you into your God-given purpose no matter what your past looks like! You can start over again. If you are someone that's a victim of a broken home and you've always wanted to have a great relationship with your family, this book is for you! Dejah Fields is an incredible writer who has lived what you are about to read. In this book she equips you to move past the pain of your past so that you can discover who God has destined you to be."
—*Lavarious A. Slaughter, Christian playwright*

Honor Yourself:
You Are Highly
Favored and Loved

Dejah Fields

Honor Yourself: You Are Highly Favored and Loved
by Dejah Fields
Copyright ©2011 Dejah Fields

Cover photographer Brian Bielmann and the photo is of Leimomi Prasser

ISBN 978-1581693683
For Worldwide Distribution
Printed in the U.S.A.

Axiom Press
P.O. Box 191540 • Mobile, AL 36619
800-367-8203

DEDICATION

This book is dedicated

to my daughter, Malia,

the strongest woman I know.

Also to Michelle DeCaul, my mentor,

who taught me to honor myself.

ACKNOWLEDGMENTS

Praise to the Holy Spirit whose enabling power and wisdom gave me the strength to press through to complete this book.

Therefore, all glory and honor goes to my Lord and Savior Jesus Christ for helping me reach my destiny.

Thank you to all my family and friends for encouraging and supporting me through this project.

now because men have stepped down from the role God intended them to fill. Women are struggling, trying to assume the role of a provider and protector that they were never meant to fill. The good news is that God has a plan to restore all that has been stolen and stripped away from His daughters.

This book has been written to help women get back to their rightful roles as God's daughters.

And they . . . shall build the old waste places:

thou shalt raise up the foundations

of many generations; and thou shalt be called,

The repairer of the breach,

The restorer of paths to dwell in.

Isaiah 58:12

guilt only to have the man you were with decide to move on to someone else?

Why would a man want you if you were like everyone else? You need to value yourself as a priceless jewel. Why would a man value you if you don't value yourself? Too many women have let men drag them through the mud. Through men's abuse, neglect, indifference, and rejection, women have been reduced to individuals who do not know who they are.

Rejection is one of the greatest fears of life. Rejection has other emotions that come right along with it—frustration, anger, hurt, low self-esteem, unworthiness, loneliness, and insecurity.

If you are putting your trust in a person, you are setting yourself up to be let down. When a woman is rejected, she will immediately take it personally. She will blame herself for what she did or what she didn't do, what she said or what she didn't say. She will feel unloved and begin questioning her appearance and look for her own personality flaws. Rejection can cause a person to isolate themselves, shut down, or just check out.

When I was in college, I had a roommate who was insecure. Every time a boy would break up with her, she would take sleeping pills and sleep for days.

When a boy stopped seeing another college friend, she would almost starve herself and eat only one hardboiled egg a day. She was certain that if she were super thin, this would never happen to her again.

Many women thought their husband would complete them as a woman. Therefore, the rejection of a spouse can be one of the most overwhelming emotions a woman will face. When the person you let into your mind, heart, and soul turns his back on you, it can be devastating. Because your dearest friend, the one with whom you have shared your most intimate thoughts, feelings, and moments has turned his back on you, the love and security you thought would last forever is now gone. The person you trusted most in this world has broken your heart. It can feel as though they have taken a part of you with them. Oftentimes the person who rejects you will not just take everything from you emotion-ally, but they may also steal your possessions. Surprisingly, many times a woman will continue to defend the person who rejected her.

I had a friend who told me her story of rejec-tion. She was married to the same man for nearly thirty years. During that time, not only was he a prominent and respected person, but would often visit churches to speak. Everyone loved and ap-

4

plauded him. My friend would sit in the pew and cringe. You see she knew his deep dark secret. He had rejected her many years ago through multiple affairs, yet he continued to keep up the appearance of righteousness. She told no one because she had a fear of losing her security. The fear of the unknown (what her life might be like alone) scared her into not wanting to make a change. She even rationalized that at least he didn't beat her.

Even her own mother told her, "It's better to have half a man than no man at all. Just keep your mouth shut. He provides well for you and the children. Why he even gave you a Mercedes!"

My friend told me her mother had accepted that type of behavior from her own husband. Hurt women who raise hurt women many times don't know their worth and therefore allow men to devalue them.

Thank God that my friend woke up one day and decided she was tired of feeling worthless, tired of lowering her standards, and tired of trying to please a man who had rejected her. She stopped believing what he said about her and started believing what the Word of God said about her.

With rejection will come many nights of blaming yourself, endless tears, and the feeling that you cannot go on. But one day when you let go and give it to God, joy will come in the morning. You will pick yourself up and move on. If a person can reject you and move out of your life, then either that person was not the one whom God intended for you or that person was not obedient to God.

Life goes on; you need to learn to move on. Although a negative experience is a bad chapter, it doesn't have to make your whole book bad.

Don't give up. The enemy wants you to think that you're nothing. He doesn't want you to trust God. He wants you to take your focus off God and onto yourself and your situation.. The enemy is after your faith. Jesus needs to be your example. He went through every imaginable pain.

Rejection can feel like a wound that will never heal. But we must remember that God is our healer and He understands rejection because He Himself experienced the pain of rejection.

> *He was despised and forsaken of men, A man of sorrows and acquainted with grief; And like one from whom men hide their face from him. He was despised and we did not esteem him. Surely He has borne our grief and carried our sorrows. Yet we did esteem him stricken and smitten by God, and afflicted. But He was wounded for our transgressions,*

6

Rejection

he was bruised for our iniquities, the chastisement of our peace was upon Him, and with HIS STRIPES WE ARE HEALED (Is. 53:3-5).

CHAPTER 2

Low Self-Esteem

L ow self-esteem basically comes from believing what others say about us instead of
what God says about us.

Our self-esteem can also be damaged by the
media. How often we compare ourselves to some
super model. So many young people today are
trying to emulate popular singers and dress a certain
way to fit that image. They watch BET or MTV
and see all the provocatively dressed females using
their bodies to attract and please a man. These females are really devaluating themselves. The sad
thing is that they may attract a man but also cause

the man to use them. But after being used and de-valued, the young girl feels like she is not good enough. So she continues to give her most prized possession away to man after man.

Every time a female has sex with a man, he takes a little piece of her; pretty soon, she hardly has anything of herself left and doesn't even know who she is anymore. This is what is meant by making soul ties with another. To go on to be a whole woman, you must repent and break these devas-tating soul ties. You need to value yourself and re-alize that a man who truly values you would not use you.

God created a woman to be a soft, tender special gift to a man. When God created Eve for Adam, He created her as an extraordinary gift to comple-ment and complete Adam.

One of my memories of wanting to be perfect was when I was in photography school studying il-lustration. I was doing a photo shoot of a young beautiful model who had the perfect figure and looks. We became good friends, and I later began to understand the price she paid for that beauty. She barely ate anything and would have to go to bed at 7:00 pm nightly with tons of creams packed on her skin and hair.

Her boyfriend, who was also her manager, was so desirous of her being a successful model that he would drive her as well. He would put her down constantly to make her want to look better. The sad part was that someone so beautiful was also very unhappy. She was always comparing herself to the models in the top selling magazines and never felt as though she would ever be as good a model as they were. She led a very lonely life and lost herself in wanting to be like someone else, instead of developing her inner beauty.

Insecurities can come from within you and from past experiences. You might have come from a family where your mom was insecure. Her identity came from your dad who had a career and was the bread winner. Since she did not have a career and didn't view all that she did to be that important, she could have tried to obtain her self-esteem from your dad.

Low self-esteem more often than not comes from those that we so much want to please. Growing up I had a brother who was not only brilliant but was also perfect. My brother would often joke that he did not know where my parents got me but that it must have been a mistake because I was so different than he was. I often got into trouble because since he did everything right, I became rebellious and purposely did everything wrong.

I often challenged my parents and teachers. I became very competitive in high school. When I didn't make the twirling squad, I took it as another indication that I was less than perfect. I didn't like myself. I wanted to be popular and skinny. When I want to college, I began to change my hairstyle, lose weight, and do anything else that I thought would make me feel better about myself. I began to believe that if I could please others, I would win their approval; and if they accepted me, I could accept myself. I wound up attracting the wrong people into my life because I wanted to fix other people and rescue them from their problems. If I could help them, they would need me, accept me, and love me.

I found myself in one dysfunctional relationship after another. It wasn't until I was in my second marriage that I realized I had lost myself in my husband. I decided to go down the road to finding out who I was. I started with finding out who God says I am. I realized I could not lower my value to someone else's level. I began to believe that I was God's daughter, "the apple of His eye" (Zech. 2:8).

The very best book I've ever read that I recommend every young woman read is *The Pursuit of Beauty* by Katie Luce. In it she talks about how young women have a lifelong search for beauty, but the sad part is that they find that beauty doesn't last.

The truth is that we will all age, and our outer beauty will fade. God knew women would have to face this; that is why He wrote in the Word, "Charm is deceitful and beauty is passing, but a woman who fears the Lord shall be praised" (Prov. 31:30, NKJV).

Katie Luce says in this book that she believes that:

God's definition of true beauty is a woman who fears the Lord, one who will give her life away for Him. When we finally give up our own ambitions, our own search for ourselves, He is free to make the heap of once useless clay into a beautiful piece of art—useful, and a joy to everyone, especially to the potter.

Katie goes on to say:

True beauty comes from God's love in our hearts. It gives sparkle to our eyes, joy and shine to our faces and energy to our bodies. It outlives our wrinkles and gray hair, giving us meaning and purpose. It gives us the ability to truly love ourselves, which empowers us to love others. We can finally take our focus off of ourselves and see this world through the eyes of God.

Thank you, Katie, for your valuable insight into the Word of God and your own personal experiences. The main message that I gained from all this is that when you put your own brokenness aside and see the broken people around you, God will use your life to deliver His message.

CHAPTER 3

Abandonment

I once was at a woman's meeting, and the woman who was ministering called out a young lady and gave her the following prophecy that I will never forget.

When I saw you, I saw a little girl waiting at a bus station, sitting on a suitcase waiting for someone you loved that was supposed to pick you up to show up. Hours passed and everyone left that bus station, but you continued to sit and wait as the tears streamed down your face. The pain grew as you realized they weren't coming. But standing behind you all the time I saw the Lord with His arms around you. He felt your hurt and saw your tears, but He never left. He says for you to use David's words, "Put my tears into Your bottle" (see Psalm 56:8, NKJV). And God is saying to you my daughter, "I will wipe away all tears from their eyes."

Even if my father and mother abandon me, the Lord will hold me close (Ps. 27:10 NLT).

I will never desert you nor forsake you (Heb. 13:5 NKJV).

This powerful message, that we have a God who loves us unconditionally and is there in our deepest pain, set this young woman free from the pain of abandonment.

Someone left. Perhaps a father or mother walked away from your family, your best friend turned their back on you, or the person you thought would be there forever abandoned you. People mess up. They are humans who get caught up in self-centered ideas and hurt others, even the people they love. It hurts. Yes, it hurts way down in your stomach until you don't think the hurt will ever go away.

A very good friend who cared about me when I was hurting sent me the following piece by T.D. Jakes.

Let It Go for 2005 by T.D. Jakes

There are people who can walk away from you.

And hear me when I tell you this!

When people can walk away from you: let them walk.

I don't want you to try to talk another person into staying with you, loving you, calling you, caring about you, coming to see you, staying attached to you.

I mean hang up the phone.

When people walk away from you, let them walk.

Your destiny is never tied to anybody that left.

The Bible said that, "They came out from us that it might be made manifest that they were not for us. For had they been of us, not doubt they would have continued with us" (1 John 2:19).

People leave you because they are not joined to you. And if they are not joined to you, you can't make them stay. Let them go.

And it doesn't mean that they are a bad person, it just means that their part in the story is over.

And you've got to know when people's part in your story is over so that you don't keep trying to raise the dead.

You've got to know then it's dead.

You've got to know then it's over.

Let me tell you something.

I've got the gift of good-bye.

It's the tenth spiritual gift, I believe in good-bye.

It's not that I'm hateful, it's that I'm faithful, and I know whatever God means for me to have, He'll give it to me.

And if it takes too much sweat, I don't need it.

Stop begging people to stay. Let them go!!

If you are holding on to something that doesn't belong to you was never intended for your life, then you need to...LET IT GO! If someone can't treat you right, love you back, and see your worth...LET IT GO! If someone has angered you...LET IT GO! If you are involve in a wrong relationship or addiction...LET IT GO! If you are holding on to a job that no longer meets you needs or talents...LET IT GO!

If you have a bad attitude...LET IT GO! If you

keep judging others to make yourself feel better...LET IT GO! If you're stuck in the past and God is trying to take you to a new level in Him...LET IT GO! If you are struggling with the healing of a broken relationship...LET IT GO!

If you keep trying to help someone who won't even try to help themselves... LET IT GO! If you're feeling depressed and stressed...LET IT GO! If there is a particular situation that you are so used to handling yourself and God is saying "take your hands off of it," then you need to...LET IT GO! Let the past be the past. Forget the former things.

God is doing a new thing for 2005!!!

LET IT GO!

Get right or get left... think about it, and then LET IT GO! The battle is the Lord's!

Many women who were abandoned by a man thought that their husband would complete them as a woman. Only God can complete you. Peace is found in God. Don't let your peace reside in people. People will love you one day and stab you in the back the next. The enemy will use emotional tactics so that all we see is the pain. You don't need to let people bring you down to their level. When you expect more than people are capable of giving you, you are setting yourself for disappointment.

Your happiness is not based on your condition but on His position. How you respond to what people do to you determines your destiny. The devil sends people to let you down. Don't let them damage your destiny. God will let things associated with you die, but he will not let you die. Read the book of Ruth. She actually extracted life out of a death situation. She took the time to see beyond her situation. You spend all your time wondering why the person you thought would have your back forever left. Stop trying to figure out why they did this to you; stop wondering if they were right or wrong. LET GO! LET GOD!

Whatever you're facing, even if it's the result of your own bad decisions, God holds your hand through it even though He doesn't stop it. You have to know that God is going to come through. He is faithful to see you through it all. Don't let fear grip your heart. Have the peace that you are going to come out of it. Turn it all over to God. MOVE ON! If you do, greatness will have a chance of coming out of you. Remember God allowed these difficult circumstances because He has a purpose for your life.

Give all your worries and cares to God, for he cares about you (1 Pet. 5:7 NLT).

For I am persuaded that neither death nor life, nor angels nor principalities nor powers, nor things present nor things to come, nor height nor depth, nor any other created thing, shall be able to separate us from the love of God which is in Christ Jesus our Lord (Rom. 8:38-9, NKJV).

HE WILL NEVER ABANDON YOU!

CHAPTER 4

Forgiveness

We live in a society where getting even and taking revenge are acceptable. Watch anything on TV, and you'll see vengeance. But what does God say?

Vengeance is Mine, says the Lord (Rom. 12:19, NKJV).

Do not be bitter or angry or mad. Never shout angrily or say things to hurt others. Never do anything evil. Be kind and loving to each other, and forgive each other just as God forgave you in Christ (Eph. 4:31-32 NCV).

Forgive? But you don't understand what he did

to me. That's what I used to say when I was living in Hawaii and my daughter's father stole her (she was only a year-and-a-half old) and took her to the mainland along with all the money I had in the bank. There was nothing I could do because at that time we were legally married. When I finally did get her back, she was devastated from the experience.

There were nights when I would actually dream of him showing up at my door, and I would open it and then blow his head off. I felt that if he were dead, he could not hurt me anymore. I was a Christian and could not understand how I could think such things. Then someone gave me a book entitled, *The Freedom of Forgiveness 70 X 7* by David Augsburger. This book was published in the 1970s, but I still have kept it and every now and then I need to read it again. I believe that this is the greatest book next to the Bible that was ever written on forgiveness.

In his book, he says:

> …forgetful forgiveness is not a case of holy amnesia which erases the past. No, instead it is the experience of healing which draws the poison from the wound.

> You may recall the hurt, but you will not relive it! No constant reviewing, no rehashing of the

old hurt, not going back to sit on the old gravestones where past grievances lie buried.

True, the hornet of memory may fly again, but forgiveness has drawn its sting. The curse is gone. The memory is powerless to arouse or anger.

Not that the past has changed. The past is the past. Nothing can alter the facts. What has happened has happened forever.

But the meaning can be changed. This is forgiveness.

Forgiveness restores the present, heals the future, and releases us from the past.

Which leads us to the final goal of forgiveness.

Beyond even forgetting, there is healing!"

Those who are in the medical profession can confirm that when people are diagnosed with serious even incurable disease, sometimes it can be rooted in anger, bitterness, and unforgiveness. When you keep this anger inside, a root of bitterness can grow. Bitterness poisons the body; it is the link between stress and illness. Fifteen chemicals are released during anger; these chemicals work on your immune system.

See to it that no one falls short of the grace of God and that no bitter root grows up to cause trouble and defile many (Heb. 12:15, NIV).

We, as humans, have the urge to get even. Unforgiveness is rooted in self-justification. After what my daughter's father did to me, the hurt I felt led to fear—the fear of being left alone. The fear in our life can manifest itself as anger. I found myself blowing up over any minor thing. At times I even took my anger out on my daughter.

Another thing that can set off outbursts of anger is blame. We blame ourselves for allowing others to hurt and abuse us. After someone hurts us, we blame ourselves for not seeing it coming. We feel guilty because of the things we have done or haven't done. We keep rehashing all the mistakes we have made and all the things we allowed them to get away with. We recall justifying things when the warning signs were there, or for making excuses for their behavior when we knew we needed to walk away. We may also now be living in the consequences of those bad choices we made. Sometimes after an extreme hurtful situation, we can make poor decisions based on emotions. Many of us have made permanent decisions (that were wrong) in temporary situations.

Destructive guilt comes from other people's standards, or is generated by Satan's accusing words. *Constructive guilt* comes from the Holy Spirit to lead us to repentance (John 16:8-11).

The way of God is to be sorry and repent. Confess your guilt to the Lord. Forgive others and yourself. Reaffirm the gospel in your life.

Augsburger says:

Revenge not only lowers you to your enemy's level; what's worse, it boomerangs. The person who seeks revenge is like a man who shoots himself in order to hit his enemy with the kick of the gun's recoil.

Revenge is the most worthless weapon in the world. It ruins the avenger while more firmly confirming the enemy in his wrong. It initiates an endless flight down the bottomless stairway of rancor, reprisals, and ruthless retaliation.

Forgiveness is not for the other person—it is for you. Forgiveness releases you. As long as you hold on to unforgiveness, that person has control over you. Some of us forgive others but forget about forgiving ourselves. Faced with the difficulties of handling our life, we begin to accept our trials as punishments for the mistakes we have made. If God has forgiven our past, why can't we?

*Who has delivered us from the power of darkness,
and hath translated us into the kingdom of his dear
son. In whom we have redemption through his
blood, even the forgiveness of sins* (Col. 1:13-14).

Augsburger says it so very well in his book:

The way to release this forgiveness begins with a
change of attitude towards you and your sins and
climaxes in a change of attitudes and actions towards God. First you must change your attitude
towards the guilt you are feeling. Examine it in
the light of the Word of God.

To release your guilt there must be true repentance. Augsburger goes on to say:

Repentance is a change of mind and heart. The
heart is not only broken for its sins, it is broken
from its sins as well.

When you are open and honest with yourself,
the person you must forgive, and God, you will have
the courage to confess your sin. Repentance equals
release. Augsburger adds:

You must turn the whole burden of blame and
the dead weight of guilt for your sin over to
God.

When we make wrong choices in our lives, we

hold ourselves responsible. We condemn ourselves and become the judge. Yes, we are responsible for what happened, but we need not condemn ourselves forever.

Fill the pain with God's love. His love will free you. He has the power to step in even if you made a mess of your life. God is not the originator of your situation, but He can fix it. He let His Son die to bring Him glory; see your situation as an opportunity He can turn around for good and bring Him glory.

If you continue to regret and go back to the mistakes you made, the devil will keep you bound. He is the "accuser of the brethren." You will give up and not move forward. If you forgive yourself and move forward, God will use your mess for a message for someone going through the same things you went through.

I have to be honest and admit that there are times when the angry thoughts, bitterness, and un-forgiveness try to come back. It happens especially when I look at my beautiful daughter and try to imagine what it must have been like for her to grow up without a father. That's when the Lord reminds me of the vision He gave me that brought me to forgiveness. In the vision, He took me to Calvary and no one was there but my daughter's father at the foot of the cross. Jesus said to me, "If he were the only person in the world, I would have died for him. I love him that much."

> *But God demonstrates his own love for us in this: While we were still sinners, Christ died for us* (Rom. 5:8, NIV).

> *But I tell you, love your enemies and pray for those who persecute you* (Matt. 5:44, NIV).

> *Then Peter came to Jesus and asked, "Lord, how many times shall I forgive my brother or sister who sins against me? Up to seven times?" Jesus answered, "I tell you, not seven times, but seventy-seven times"* (Matt. 18:21-22, NIV).

CHAPTER 5

Freedom

H old on! The morning is coming. Don't let where you are today be where you stay. Your strength of character is developed in those lonely dark times when you endure. Hold your peace, your endurance will make room for your breakthrough. Jesus is close to the brokenhearted. Is there anything too hard for God? Hold on to your peace; your endurance will make room for your breakthrough.

Many are the afflictions of the righteous, but the Lord delivers us out of them all (Ps. 34:19).

When all you see is the pain, remember God's unconditional love.

Behold, I am the LORD, the God of all flesh. Is there anything too hard for Me? (Jer. 32:27, NKJV)

Release it all to God. You never have to cry about it again. Change the way you think. Spend time with God. When you wrap yourself in His Word, it will bring healing and deliverance. There is nothing He can't get you out of. He will work everything out. He will put back the broken pieces of your life and set up godly connections in your life.

You need to trust God. He knows what you need and knows your destiny. Your future is in the hands of a mighty God.

He has made everything beautiful in His time (Ecc. 3:11, NKJV).

When you see what God can do, you'll forget the pain. What the enemy meant for evil, God will turn around for your good (Rom. 8:28). God will make the crooked way straight. You will recover all, and He will give you better.

The LORD will make you the head, not the tail...
you will always be at the top, never at the bottom
(Deut. 28:13, NIV).

You will have a new beginning; the devil can't stop your blessing. The same spirit that raised

Christ from the dead dwells in you (see Rom. 8:11). He will restore you when you are depleted. He will strengthen you and put your life back together. Don't let fear grip your heart. Find a promise for your problem.

He says, "Fear Not" in one way or another 365 times in the Bible.

So do not fear, for I am with you (Is. 41:10, NIV).

For God has not given us a spirit of fear, but of power and of love and of a sound mind (2 Tim. 1:17, NKJV).

Moreover David said, "The LORD, who delivered me from the paw of the lion and from the paw of the bear, He will deliver me from the hand of this Philistine" (1 Sam. 17:37).

Everything is possible for one who believes (Mark 9:23).

You need to throw away the memory of the person who hurt you. Cut off dead things and people in your life and let go of the people who bring you down. Don't allow your past failures to possess you. You can't go forward looking back. People will talk about your past, but God talks about your potential. The same people who tried to hold you down will wonder how you got up there.

. . . but one thing I do, forgetting those things which are behind and reaching forward to those things which are ahead . . . (Phil. 3:13, NKJV).

When one season is over, another is beginning. You will go from struggling to soaring. Everything that has happened to you is under the blood. Don't believe what others have said about you, believe the word of God.

For I know the thoughts that I think toward you, says the LORD, thoughts of peace and not of evil, to give you a future and a hope (Jer. 29:11, NKJV).

Keep your mind stayed on Jesus. Confess, "I put myself in agreement with God's Word." You need to command peace in your life. Your peace does not come from a person. Never let yourself need someone more than God.

You need to be whole. You cannot reach your potential until you realize your value. My favorite scripture in the Bible is Psalm 138:8:

The LORD will perfect that which concerns me....

God has the power to fix your life. For things to change you have to change. Take control of your thought life. Renew your mind.

A new heart I will give you (Eze. 36:26).

Life will always come to you according to your expectations. Expect blessings from God.

The glory of this latter temple shall be greater than the former (Haggai 2:9).

See yourself as God sees you: powerful and anointed. He says that He has named you victorious and loved.

Embrace yourself. Love yourself as God loves you. Remind yourself of who you are and whose you are.

I have loved you with an everlasting love (Jer. 31:3, NKJV).

You are His masterpiece; you were created in His image.

. . . give attention to my words . . . Keep them in the midst of your heart (Prov. 4:20-21, NKJV).

He says to you, "Lift up your eyes my daughter, not longer will you weep, I will carry your cares."

Be still and know that I am God (Ps. 46:10).

If one person falls, the other can reach out and help (Ecc. 4:10, NLT).

You need a mentor—someone who will hold

you up, speak life over you, and have your back. A mentor will push you to the next level and protect what's inside of you.

During one of my lowest times, God gave me just that kind of person. She would encourage me, pray for me, and speak the Word over me. When I was weak, I would feed off her faith. She taught me that I was a "jewel of Christ" and needed to value myself. She saw the destiny that God had for me and helped to push greatness out of me. Now she rejoices with me that God has inspired me to write this book. My mentor taught me a valuable truth,

> *What we go through is not for us,*
> *it's to help someone else.*

In summary, flowers, which are so beautiful and admired by many, enhance the world that we live in. Flowers serve a variety of purposes to enhance our lives. For us as women, we love to receive perfume and fragrances as gifts, but how often do we ponder or understand the process a flower goes through to be displayed? The fragrances that we use in our home were hand selected and collected in order to produce the smell of our favorite fragrance. After the flower is hand selected, it goes through a crushing, steaming, and extraction process to bring out the scents and aromatic fragrances that make it pleasant for people.

It is important to realize that as a woman we are like that flower that goes through the crushing process. We may not understand why certain situations happen in our lives. But if we look at a flower and understand the process for it to become an aromatic bottle of perfume for all to enjoy, we realize that God has the same plan for us.

It is not until we have experienced a little turbulence or hardship in our lives that we experience our "fragrance." A flower's fragrance will not be released until it is crushed! So our crushing is all a part of the process to bring forth our beauty, strength, and wisdom. So rather than wither away, wilt, or get dried up like some flowers, we need to embrace the process of becoming an aromatic irresistible fragrance! The fragrance we release will attract many to inquire and understand how we endured our process. Then and only then, will we have the greatest opportunity to share and help another woman to go through her "flowering" process.

So celebrate your journey and align your words to what God has called you to do and be! Allow your journey to begin with: 1) making a choice to live in freedom, 2) choosing to forgive those that hurt you, 3) connecting with those that celebrate you, 5) dismissing every negative thought with the Word of God, and 6) identifying your purpose and living in it!

EPILOGUE

My prayer is that this book has been a helpful tool to direct you to the very Word of God that will make you free from the hurts and pain that have attacked your very soul. I know from my own personal experience that when those I thought would love me and be there for me forever continually abused, rejected, and abandoned me, it was only the love of God that lifted me back up. I remember the times when it hurt so bad that I thought I would never face another day.

There was a dark season when I all I could do was lay in bed and hold my Bible but JOY COMES IN THE MORNING! Praise God, there was one day when I got up and said, "Enough is enough!" I was tired of being sick and tired. God raised me up and showed me that my destiny was greater than my current circumstances. My pain and hurt pushed me to write this book. The Lord said to me, "Lift up your eyes, my daughter. No longer will you have to weep; I will carry your cares."

He showed me that I was meant to HONOR MYSELF, because I WAS HIGHLY FAVORED AND LOVED!

ABOUT THE AUTHOR

Dejah Fields holds a Masters degree in biblical counseling and education. She is known for her beloved book, *Mama I Want To Be Like You.* Not only is she respected as an author but also as a teacher and motivational speaker. She has a burden to help women know who they are in Christ and totally fall in love with Jesus. Her desire is to see all women value and love themselves as their heavenly Father values and loves them, to recognize their potential, fulfill their purpose, reach their destiny, and to live Psalm 30 (AMP), "His favor is life, or in His favor is life. Weeping may endure for a night, but JOY comes in the morning. You have turned my mourning into dancing for me!"

Contact Information

The author would love to hear from her readers. If you would like to send her a note or contact her to book a speaking engagement or to obtain more copies of this book, email her at Dejah05@gmail.com.